Grammar
Practice Book

Grade 2

Harcourt
SCHOOL PUBLISHERS

www.harcourtschool.com

ISBN 10   0-15-349909-5
ISBN 13   978-0-15-349909-8

   14 15 16 17   0982   15 14 13 12 11
4500303728

Contents

Contents

Name _____

▶ **Read each group of words. If the group is a sentence, write *sentence*. If it is not a sentence, write *no*.**

1. a small cat _____

2. My family wants a cat. _____

3. a red apple _____

4. Arthur's best friend _____

5. I can ride a bike. _____

6. I want to go to the library. _____

7. want new books _____

8. Dan wrote me a letter. _____

Grammar Practice Book
© Harcourt • Grade 2

► **Put each group of words together in sentence order. Then write the sentence correctly.**

1. thirsty.   My cat   was

   _____

2. My family   a picture.   took

   _____

3. a pet.   Arthur   wants

   _____

4. We   on a picnic.   went

   _____

5. a letter.   My grandmother   sent

   _____

Grammar Practice Book

Name _____

▶ **Circle each sentence that is written correctly.**

1. that cat sat on my hat

2. This book is heavy.

3. her family I met

4. The girl ran home.

5. jan made a sandwich

▶ **Now write the other sentences correctly. Begin each one with a capital letter and end each sentence with a period.**

6. _____

7. _____

8. _____

Name _____

▶ **Read each group of words. If the group is a sentence, write *sentence* on the line. If it is not a sentence, write *no*.**

1. I see a frog. _____

2. jumped the frog in the water _____

3. Pat sat on the rug. _____

4. Ann and Dan can run fast. _____

5. cakes and cookies _____

▶ **Write each group of words as a complete sentence. Put the words in correct sentence order.**

6. blue house I live in a

_____

7. next to mine is your house

_____

8. my street is on my school

_____

▶ **Read each group of words. If the group
is a statement, write *statement*. If it is a
question, write *question*.**

1. Frog rakes leaves. _____

2. Where does Frog live? _____

3. Does Toad live in a house? _____

4. I wish I lived near them. _____

▶ **Write each group of words as a complete sentence. Begin
with a capital letter. End with a period or a question mark.**

5. the bus stop is on the corner

   _____

6. how do you get to school

   _____

7. i want to ride on the school bus

   _____

8. have you ever been on an airplane

   _____

Name 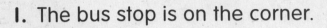 _____

▶ **Read each statement. Then write the
question it answers.**

1. The bus stop is on the corner.

_____

2. I walk to school every day.

_____

3. I never ride the school bus.

_____

4. Brad is going to visit his grandmother.

_____

5. My grandmother drives a big car.

_____

Grammar Practice Book
© Harcourt • Grade 2

▶ **Write each sentence. Add the correct end mark to show whether it is a question or a statement.**

1. Frog is my best friend

_____

2. Did Toad rake your leaves

_____

3. I wish Frog lived near me

_____

4. I would like to visit him

_____

5. Would you come with me

_____

Grammar Practice Book
© Harcourt • Grade 2

Name _____

▶ **Write the correct end mark on the line.**

1. Where are you going _____

2. I am going to a birthday party _____

3. The party is for my friend Anna _____

4. Do you know how old she is _____

5. She is eight years old _____

▶ **Write each sentence correctly.**

6. i have two brothers

_____

7. i have one sister

_____

8. do you have any brothers or sisters

_____

Grammar Practice Book
© Harcourt • Grade 2

Name _____

▶ **Read each sentence. If it is a command, write *command*. If the sentence is an exclamation, write *exclamation*.**

1. I want a pet! _____

2. Dad and Mom said yes! _____

3. Please take me to find a pet. _____

4. Come and see the dogs. _____

5. This is the one for me! _____

6. Please buy this one. _____

7. At last I have a dog! _____

8. Mudge is huge! _____

Grammar Practice Book
© Harcourt • Grade 2

▶ **Write each sentence correctly. Begin with
a capital letter. End with a period or an
exclamation mark.**

1. let's play in the park

_____

2. look at that tall slide

_____

3. please take your brother to the sandbox

_____

4. let's leave in ten minutes

_____

5. look how far I can jump

_____

Name _____

▶ **Read the paragraph. Write one statement, one question, one command, and one exclamation from the paragraph.**

> Today is cleanup day. Does your family have cleanup day? My mom tells us what to do. "Pick up your toys. Make your bed. Take out the trash." Sometimes I just want to play!

1. statement _____

_____

2. question _____

_____

3. command _____

_____

4. exclamation _____

Grammar Practice Book
© Harcourt • Grade 2

Name _____

▶ **Read each sentence. If it is a statement,
write *statement*.
If it is a question, write *question*.
If it is a command, write *command*.
If it is an exclamation, write *exclamation*.**

1. Get your backpacks. _____

2. It is time to go to school. _____

3. Oh, the bus is coming! _____

4. Do you want to be late? _____

5. Pick up your lunch box. _____

▶ **Write each sentence correctly.**

6. please water the plants

_____

7. look at the huge flower on my plant

_____

12

Name _____

▶ **Complete each sentence by writing a naming part.**

1. _____ has a dog.

2. _____ is my dog's name.

3. _____ can play the piano.

4. _____ sings to my dog.

▶ **Complete each sentence by writing a telling part.**

5. My dog _____

6. Carlos _____

7. Kate and Dan _____

8. We _____

13

▶ **Use the word *and* to join the naming parts of each pair of sentences. Write the new sentence.**

1. My friend walked home. I walked home.

   _____

2. The turtle swam in the pond. The fish swam in the pond.

   _____

   _____

3. Ann built a sand castle. Tori built a sand castle.

   _____

4. The lion roared. The tiger roared.

   _____

5. Molly picked flowers. I picked flowers.

   _____

Name _____

▶ **If the naming part of the sentence is underlined, write *naming*. Then write the sentence with a different naming part. If the telling part of the sentence is underlined, write *telling*. Write the sentence with a different telling part.**

1. I walked to Ana's house. _____

_____

2. We played with the dog. _____

_____

3. My mom came to get me. _____

_____

4. We bought some dog food. _____

_____

15

► **Match each naming part with a telling part. Write a complete sentence.**

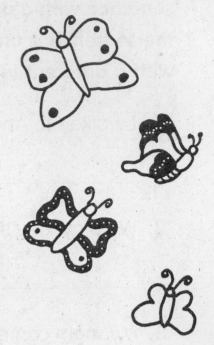

Naming Part	Telling Part
Butterflies	work hard.
Ants	make honey.
Spiders	fly.
Bees	make webs.

1. _____

2. _____

3. _____

4. _____

Grammar Practice Book
© Harcourt • Grade 2

Name _____

▶ **Circle each group of words that is a complete sentence.**

1. Maria is my best friend.

2. We like to do things together.

3. Skipping rocks on the pond.

4. Lin and I go fishing at the lake.

5. Close to my house.

6. Ken and Tino play on the same team.

▶ **Read each statement. Then write the question it answers.**

7. A puppy is a baby dog.

_____

8. My birthday is June 1.

_____

Grammar Practice Book
© Harcourt • Grade 2

▶ **Read each sentence. Write whether it is a**
statement, a _question_, a _command_, or an
exclamation.

1. It's pouring rain outside! _____

2. Close the windows. _____

3. Will my bike get wet? _____

4. Rain is good for the flowers. _____

▶ **Read each sentence. Underline the naming part of each**
sentence once. Underline the telling part twice.

5. Sam and Ann bought new bikes.

6. They rode on the bike trail.

7. I read a new book.

8. Mom and I love books.

Name _____

▶ **Circle the nouns in each sentence.**

1. James hopes to be a fireman.

2. That job takes courage.

3. Fire stations sometimes have dogs.

4. The men rush to put out the fire.

5. The firefighters try to save the building.

▶ **Read the following groups of words.**
Write the noun in each group.

6. ball, slow, deep _____

7. boy, sad, tall _____

8. graze, horses, trot _____

9. hopping, fast, mailboxes _____

10. soccer, kicked, white _____

Grammar Practice Book
© Harcourt • Grade 2

Name _____

▶ Fill in the chart. Write two examples for each kind of noun.

People	Places	Animals	Things
1. _____	3. _____	5. _____	7. _____
2. _____	4. _____	6. _____	8. _____

▶ Choose four nouns from the chart above. Write two sentences. Use two of the nouns in each sentence.

_____

_____

_____

_____

20

Name _____

▶ **Choose four things in your classroom.**
Write the noun that names each thing.

1. _____

2. _____

3. _____

4. _____

▶ **Think of four places you know. Write the noun that**
names each place.

5. _____

6. _____

7. _____

8. _____

21

Grammar Practice Book
© Harcourt • Grade 2

Name _____

▶ **Find the noun in each sentence.**
   Write it on the line.

1. The field is big. _____

2. Mia plays hard. _____

3. The score is close. _____

4. There is my team. _____

▶ **Read the following sentences. Fill in each blank with a noun.**

5. Buddy is my _____.

6. _____ is going now.

7. A small _____ is running away.

8. My _____ is broken.

Grammar Practice Book
© Harcourt • Grade 2

▶ **Complete each sentence. Change the noun in ( ) to name more than one. Write the plural noun on the line.**

1. Gus and I have to finish our _____. (chore)

2. Then we can ride our _____. (bike)

3. Gus and I like to play on the _____, too. (swing)

4. We watch the _____ on the lake. (duck)

5. Be quiet, we might see _____ nearby. (bunny)

6. After dinner, we have to wash the _____. (dish)

7. Aunt Lisa always brings us _____ from her travels. (toy)

8. Gus and I are good _____. (buddy)

Grammar Practice Book
© Harcourt • Grade 2

Name _____

▶ **Draw a line from each singular word to its matching plural.**

1. child   feet

2. man   mice

3. foot   children

4. mouse   women

5. tooth   men

6. woman   teeth

▶ **Write sentences using two of the plural words above.**

7. _____

8. _____

Grammar Practice Book
© Harcourt • Grade 2

▶ **Read each sentence. Circle the nouns.**

1. The boy is learning to ride his bike.

2. My friend wants to ride to the park.

3. My father rode beside the girl and her brother.

4. My family will drive our car to their house.

▶ **Write the nouns that you circled in the sentences above in
their plural forms.**

5. _____ , _____

6. _____ , _____

7. _____ , _____ , _____

8. _____ , _____ , _____

Grammar Practice Book
© Harcourt • Grade 2

▶ **Underline each plural noun in the sentences below.**

1. The children will plant tulips in the garden.

2. The adults are going to plant roses.

3. The garden will have many pretty flowers.

4. I think we should plant trees too.

▶ **Think of new plural nouns to replace the ones in the sentences above. Write each new sentence.**

5. _____

6. _____

7. _____

8. _____

Grammar Practice Book
© Harcourt • Grade 2

Write each sentence correctly. Begin each proper noun with a capital letter.

1. Would you like to go to the ball game, mr. allen?

_____

_____

2. It is at the park on crane street.

_____

3. My friends carol and marcy will be there.

_____

_____

4. My aunt rose will bring hot dogs.

_____

5. My aunt is from the state of virginia.

_____

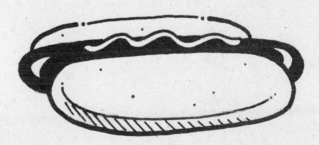

Name _____

▶ **Circle the sentences that are written correctly.**

1. mrs. brown brought her cat, muffy, to the park.

2. Olivia played with her dog, Max.

3. Mr. Juarez ran with his dog, Spot.

4. connor played catch with his dog, perry.

5. ms. james brushed her cat, ashley.

▶ **Write the other sentences correctly.**

6. _____

   _____

7. _____

8. _____

▶ **Write each proper name correctly.**

1. mr. howard jameson _____

2. miss tara wilkes _____

3. mrs. yuliana perez _____

4. mr. james cuva _____

▶ **Answer each question with a complete sentence. Begin each proper noun with a capital letter.**

5. What is the name of your school?

_____

6. Who is your principal?

_____

7. What is your full name?

_____

8. What is your address?

_____

▶ **Read each group of words below. If the words are proper nouns, write *proper noun*. If they are not proper nouns, write *no*.**

1. Mr. Tibbs _____

2. Elm Street _____

3. pretty birds _____

4. Stacey _____

5. Heritage Elementary School _____

6. my friend _____

▶ **Write each sentence correctly. Begin each proper noun with a capital letter.**

7. bessie took her pet snake, buddy, to show and tell.

_____

_____

8. My pet bird, tiny, can say five words.

_____

Grammar Practice Book
© Harcourt • Grade 2

Name _____

▶ **Fill in the blank with the correct proper noun.**

1. Monday, Tuesday, _____

2. March, _____, May

3. _____, September, October

4. Thursday, Friday, _____

5. January, February, _____

6. _____, Saturday, Sunday

7. May, June, _____

8. November, _____, January

Grammar Practice Book
© Harcourt • Grade 2

▶ **Write the proper nouns correctly.**

1. thursday, november 9 _____

2. monday, april 24 _____

3. friday, june 8 _____

4. tuesday, september 21 _____

5. sunday, december 29 _____

▶ **Write each sentence correctly.**

6. valentine's day is february 14th.

_____

7. We celebrate independence day on july 4th.

_____

_____

8. new year's day is on january 1st.

_____

Grammar Practice Book
© Harcourt • Grade 2

Name _____

▶ **Circle the proper nouns in the paragraph.
Write them correctly on the lines below.**

Everyone on our farm likes to celebrate the fourth of july.
Every year, uncle james gets fireworks. We have a big cookout
at prairie trail park. We even bring our dogs, tex and bella. We
do not go to bed until after we see the fireworks. It does not
matter if it is a tuesday or a saturday because we're on summer
vacation!

1. _____

2. _____

3. _____

4. _____

5. _____

6. _____

7. _____

Grammar Practice Book
© Harcourt • Grade 2

▶ **Look at the picture clue. Write the matching holiday from the box. Begin each proper noun with a capital letter.**

| groundhog day | valentine's day | mother's day |
| thanksgiving | presidents' day | veterans day |

1. _____

2. _____

3. _____

4. _____

5. _____

6. _____

Grammar Practice Book
© Harcourt • Grade 2

Name _____

▶ **Circle all the nouns in the sentences.**

   1. George and Martha read a book.

   2. Two boys were in a boat at a lake.

   3. Their boat got stuck on the sand.

   4. Water spilled into the boat.

   5. The boys in the story decided to walk home.

▶ **Complete each sentence with a plural noun.**

   6. I like to collect _____.

   7. The cook bakes tasty _____.

   8. My dad works with _____.

   9. The house has many _____.

35

Name _____

▶ **Read each group of words. Write the proper noun correctly.**

1. saturday, weekend, day _____

2. flag day, songs, celebrate _____

3. summer, july, hot _____

4. spring, rainy, march _____

5. weekday, thursday, afternoon _____

6. picnic, holiday, labor day _____

▶ **Write the place names correctly.**

7. tampa, florida _____

8. san diego, california _____

9. dallas, texas _____

10. chicago, illinois _____

Grammar Practice Book
© Harcourt • Grade 2

Name _____

▶ **Read each word. Write *yes*, if it is an abbreviation. Write *no*, if it is not an abbreviation.**

1. Jamaica _____

2. Sat. _____

3. Mrs. _____

4. Mon. _____

5. Thursday _____

6. Dr. _____

7. Tues. _____

8. Friday _____

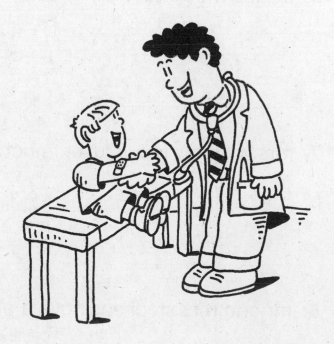

Grammar Practice Book
© Harcourt • Grade 2

▶ **Write the correct abbreviation for each month or day.**

1. Sunday _____

2. November _____

3. September _____

4. Tuesday _____

5. January _____

▶ **Write the sentences correctly.**

6. ms lee made cookies for us.

_____

_____

7. mrs williams is our favorite baby-sitter.

_____

_____

8. mr and mrs stephens have a party every year.

_____

_____

Name _____

▶ **Circle the correct abbreviation for each word.**

1. March   Mr.   Mon.   Mar.

2. Wednesday   Wdsy.   Wed.   Wedn.

3. February   Fri.   Fbry.   Feb.

4. December   Dec.   Thurs.   Dmbr.

▶ **Read each item below. Rewrite each item, using abbreviations correctly.**

5. jan 16 _____

6. mr anthony martin _____

7. mon, dec 29 _____

8. dr joy hardin _____

▶ **Read the paragraph. Write the correct abbreviation for each day and month.**

Fall

I love the fall. Every **(1)** September, **(2)** October, and **(3)** November, the weather is so nice and cool. On **(4)** Saturday and **(5)** Sunday my family spends a lot of time outdoors. We know that **(6)** December, **(7)** January, and **(8)** February will bring very cold weather.

1. _____

2. _____

3. _____

4. _____

5. _____

6. _____

7. _____

8. _____

► **Read each sentence. If it has a possessive noun, circle the noun and write *possessive noun* on the line. If it doesn't have a possessive noun, write *no*.**

1. Long ago, my grandfather played baseball.

   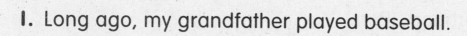

2. My grandmother's favorite game was tennis.

   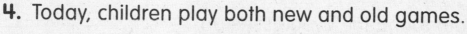

3. Brady's favorite game is basketball.

   _____

4. Today, children play both new and old games.

   _____

5. My dad's favorite game is marbles.

   _____

6. My mother's hobby is making clay pots.

   _____

Grammar Practice Book
© Harcourt • Grade 2

Name _____

▶ **Complete each sentence. Change the noun
in ( ) to show ownership, and write it on
the line.**

1. We went for a walk in _____
   neighborhood. (Pam)

2. We went to see _____ new house.
   (Mrs. Stout)

3. She was looking for _____ eyeglasses.
   (Mr. Stout)

4. Are they under _____ pillow? (Peggy)

5. Are they in _____ toy box? (Bobby)

6. Mrs. Stout found the eyeglasses on

   _____ dresser. (Mr. Stout)

Grammar Practice Book
© Harcourt • Grade 2

Name _Oliver_

▶ **Read each group of words. Then write it
with a possessive noun.**

   1. the house of Tony _____

   2. the skateboard that belongs to Tim _____

   3. the bone that belongs to Fido _____

   4. the backpack that belongs to Marcia _____

▶ **Write each sentence so that the noun in ( )
shows ownership.**

   5. (Mr. Franklin) dog was lost.

   _____

   6. We checked (Mrs. Brown) yard.

   _____

   7. We looked in (the mailman) yard, too.

   _____

   8. The dog was under (Mr. Franklin) car the whole time!

   _____

   _____

43

▶ **Follow the directions to write the possessive form of each noun.**

   1. American + apostrophe + *s*

_____

   2. country + apostrophe + *s*

_____

   3. eagle + apostrophe + *s*

_____

   4. flag + apostrophe + *s*

_____

   5. George Washington + apostrophe + *s*

_____

▶ **Write sentences for three of the possessive nouns you wrote above.**

   6. _____

   7. _____

   8. _____

Name _____

▶ **Write a verb from the box that best
completes each sentence.**

decide	listen	opens	talks

1. Robin _____ about the new park.

2. The town leaders _____ what to do.

3. They _____ to what the people want.

4. The park _____ on the Fourth of July.

▶ **Write each sentence. Use the correct verb in ( ).**

5. The council (serve, serves) the people.

_____

6. Many towns (elect, elects) a mayor.

_____

7. We (vote, votes) every two years.

_____

Grammar Practice Book
© Harcourt • Grade 2

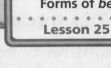

Name _____

▶ **Read each verb that tells about now. Change the verb to make it tell about the past.**

I. walk _____

2. deliver _____

3. mix _____

4. want _____

5. ask _____

▶ **Circle the form of *be* in each sentence. Write now if the verb is in the present-tense form. Write past if the verb is in the past-tense form.**

6. I am excited! _____

7. My friends and I were late. _____

8. Sara is happy. _____

9. Maddy was at the store. _____

10. We are shopping. _____

Name _____

▶ **Circle the verb in ( ) that best completes each sentence. Write it on the line.**

1. Yung (had, have) _____ a dream about a New York bagel.

2. Now Yung must (have, has) _____ a bagel.

3. He (has, have) _____ an idea.

4. The pigeon (have, has) _____ the note in his carrier.

5. Farmer Ahn (had, have) _____ a plow wheel.

6. Fisherman Kee (have, had) _____ a life ring.

7. Beekeeper Lee (had, have) _____ a swarm of bees.

8. Now Yung can (has, have) _____ his bagel!

9. I once (has, had) _____ dreams about food.

10. My brother (has, have) _____ never tried bagels.

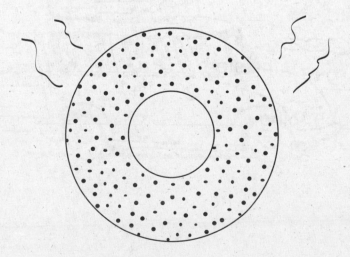

Grammar Practice Book
© Harcourt • Grade 2

Name _____

▶ **These sentences tell about now. Write *has* or *have* on each line.**

1. I _____ a suitcase.

2. My brother _____ a backpack.

3. We _____ all the things we need for our trip.

4. Do you _____ what you need?

▶ **These sentences tell about the past. Underline the subject of each sentence. Then write *had* to complete each sentence.**

5. We _____ a good time on our trip.

6. I _____ fun at my grandmother's house.

7. My sister _____ a lot of fun at the party.

8. My grandfather _____ four fishing poles last year.

Grammar Practice Book
© Harcourt • Grade 2

▶ **Write each sentence, using the correct verb in ( ).**

1. Elmer (has, have) a swimming lesson today.

_____

2. He (have, has) everything ready.

_____

3. I (have, has) my lesson today, too.

_____

4. My tent (had, has) a hole in it last week.

_____

5. My mom (have, had) to get me a new tent.

_____

▶ **Look at the picture of the campers. Write three sentences. Use the verbs has, had, and have.**

6. _____

7. _____

8. _____

Grammar Practice Book
© Harcourt • Grade 2

Name _____

▶ **Read each sentence. If *has*, *had*, or *have* is used correctly, write *yes*. If the verb is not used correctly, write *no*.**

1. I has a bucket. _____

2. I have a shovel, too. _____

3. We had fun this morning. _____

4. We has a picnic on the sand. _____

5. Jasmine have seven seashells. _____

▶ **Rewrite the sentences that are incorrect above. Write them correctly on the lines.**

6. _____

7. _____

8. _____

Grammar Practice Book
© Harcourt • Grade 2

Name _____

► **Read each sentence. Underline the verb.**
If the verb is present tense, write *now*. If the
verb is past tense, write *past*.

1. Gabriela Mistral gave herself her own name.

   _____

2. As a little girl, she saw words and learned to read.

   _____

3. She sees the Andes mountains from her window. _____

4. Sofia and Ana came to Gabriela's pretend school. _____

5. Pedro must go to school to learn his ABCs. _____

6. Today, Gabriela gives speeches to teachers. _____

7. She goes to countries all over the world. _____

8. Teachers come from everywhere to learn from her.

   _____

95

Name _____

► **Complete the chart with the correct form of each irregular verb. The first one is done for you.**

Irregular Verb	Present or Now	Past
come	come, comes	came
run	_____	ran
give	give, gives	_____
go	_____	went
do	_____	did
see	see, sees	_____

Grammar Practice Book
© Harcourt • Grade 2

Name _____

▶ **Read the words under each line. Choose the verb that tells about now. Write it on the line.**

1. Rosa _____ to her cousin's house.
   (runs, ran)

2. She and Jose _____ for a walk.
   (go, went)

3. They _____ a new trail.
   (see, saw)

4. They _____ not follow it.
   (do, did)

▶ **Read each sentence that tells about now. Rewrite the sentence to tell about the past.**

5. My uncle goes to Spain.

   _____

6. He sees many beautiful flowers.

   _____

7. He comes to our house after each trip.

   _____

Grammar Practice Book
© Harcourt • Grade 2

Name _____

▶ **Read each sentence. Draw one line under the verbs that tell about now and two lines under the verbs that tell about the past.**

1. We go on a hike.

2. We run down the hills.

3. David came with us.

4. We saw fossils in the sand.

▶ **5.–8. Rewrite the story. Make each verb tell about now.**

We came to Sunset Trail. Jake ran ahead of us.
He saw a squirrel. We went to see the squirrel, too.

_____

_____

_____

▶ **Read each sentence. If the sentence has a helping verb, circle it and write *yes*. If it does not have a helping verb, write *no*.**

1. People have collected rocks for years. _____

2. Rocks are everywhere. _____

3. I have saved many interesting rocks. _____

4. James had found an igneous rock, but he lost it.

   _____

5. He has found sedimentary rocks, too. _____

6. Metamorphic rocks are another type of rock. _____

7. Limestone is a type of sedimentary rock. _____

8. I have collected rocks for a long time. _____

9. Igneous rocks are made by heat. _____

10. Some rocks feel soft. _____

Grammar Practice Book
© Harcourt • Grade 2

▶ **Read the sentences. Circle the main verb. Underline the helping verb.**

1. I have collected baseball cards since I was five.

2. Gail has collected hats for a while.

3. Many people have found things to collect.

4. I had thought about collecting stamps, but I changed my mind.

▶ **Read the sentences. Write the present-tense helping verb that completes each sentence. Then rewrite each sentence using the past-tense helping verb.**

5. Mr. Ash _____ come to the show.

   _____

6. Sadie _____ made cookies to bring.

   _____

7. I _____ spent all of my money.

   _____

8. John _____ made all the puppets.

   _____

Name _____

▶ **Read the words under each line. Choose the correct helping verb to complete the sentence. Write it on the line.**

1. Jimmy _____ brought his coin collection to school.
    (have, has)

2. Angel _____ collected teddy bears.
    (has, have)

3. Trudy _____ gone with her aunt to the museum.
    (has, have)

4. I _____ not started a collection, yet.
    (has, have)

5. I _____ thought about collecting books.
    (have, has)

6. My mom _____ saved some of my favorite picture books.

101

Name _____

▶ **Rewrite each sentence, adding the helping verb *have* or *has*.**

1. Josh brought his bike to the store.

_____

2. He bought a special box.

_____

3. I used a box for my toy cars.

_____

4. My cars stayed together in the box.

_____

▶ **Write each sentence. Use the correct helping verb in ( ).**

5. My father (have, has) given my mother a diamond ring.

_____

6. I (has, have) tried it on.

_____

7. My mother (has, have) worn it for years.

_____

8. I (has, have) always dreamed of wearing a diamond ring

someday.

_____

Name _____

► **Complete the chart by writing the contraction for each word pair.**

Verb	Not	Contraction
do	not	1. _____
did	not	2. _____
had	not	3. _____
has	not	4. _____
can	not	5. _____
are	not	6. _____
is	not	7. _____
was	not	8. _____

103

Grammar Practice Book
© Harcourt • Grade 2

▶ **Read the sentences. On each line, write the two words that make up the underlined contraction.**

1. A long time ago, the sun <u>didn't</u> come out. _____

2. The animals <u>couldn't</u> find it. _____

3. The lizard <u>wouldn't</u> stop looking for it. _____

4. The sun <u>doesn't</u> want to wake up. _____

▶ **Rewrite each sentence. Use a contraction in place of the underlined words.**

5. I <u>do not</u> know if it will be sunny today.

   _____

6. We <u>are not</u> going to the movies.

   _____

7. Jason <u>does not</u> know that it is time to go home.

   _____

Name _____

▶ **Read each sentence. Underline the contraction. Write the two words that make up the contraction.**

1. The frogs and the toads didn't find the sun. _____

2. The fish and the turtles couldn't find the sun. _____

3. The deer and the squirrels can't find the sun. _____

4. I don't know where to look for the sun. _____

5. The rabbits and hares haven't found the sun. _____

▶ **Write three sentences. Use three of the contractions from above.**

6. _____

7. _____

8. _____

105

Name _____

▶ **Read the paragraph. Make a contraction with the words in ( ). Write it on the line.**

I (would not) **(I)** _____ like it if the sun did

not come up. I (do not) **(2)** _____ like it

when it is cold and dark. At those times, I (can not) **(3)**

_____ see the flowers and trees. I am glad that

the sun (does not) **(4)** _____ really disappear!

▶ **Write the two words that make up the contraction found in each sentence.**

5. Arlene Jameson hasn't gone to the lake.

_____

6. She doesn't know how to get there. _____

7. The Jamesons weren't going to the lake.

_____

8. We can't take Arlene with us. _____

▶ **Write each sentence. Use the correct verb in ( ).**

1. Jenny (have, has) pictures from her trip.

_____

2. Pat (goes, went) to the beach last year.

_____

3. I like to (run, ran) on the beach.

_____

4. We (do, does) many things on vacation.

_____

▶ **Read the sentences that tell about now. Rewrite them to tell about the past.**

5. Terry runs after a butterfly.

_____

6. Nicki sees the mountains.

_____

7. Jessie goes surfing.

_____

Grammar Practice Book
© Harcourt • Grade 2

▶ **Read the sentences. Circle the main verb. Underline the helping verb.**

1. My family has visited the Grand Canyon.

2. We have hiked in the mountains.

3. Dad had climbed to the top.

▶ **Rewrite each sentence. Add the helping verb *have* or *has*.**

4. Beth walked on the path.

_____

5. I skipped down the trail.

_____

▶ **Read the sentences. On each line, write the two words that make up the underlined contraction.**

6. I <u>don't</u> want to miss the show. _____

7. We <u>didn't</u> buy the tickets. _____

8. We <u>aren't</u> leaving yet. _____

INDEX

A

Abbreviations, 37–40, 53
Action verbs, 73–76, 89
Adjectives, 55–58, 59–62, 63–66,
  67–70, 71–72
  comparing with, 67–70, 72
  number words, 63–66, 72
  senses, 59–62, 71
  tell what kind, 55–58, 71
Apostrophes
  in contractions, 103–106, 108
  in possessive nouns, 41–44, 45–48,
   53–54

B

Be **(verb)**, 85–88, 90

C

Capitalization
  names of days, months, and
   holidays, 31–34, 36
  names of people, places, and
   animals, 27–30, 35–36
  proper nouns, 27–30, 31–34, 36
  sentences, 1–4, 5–8, 9–12
  titles for people, 37–40
Combining parts of sentences,
  14, 74
Commands, 9–12, 18

Common nouns, 19–22, 23–26, 35
Complete sentences, 1–4, 5–8, 9–12,
  13–16, 17–18
  See also Sentences, kinds of
Contractions, 103–106, 108

E

End marks, 1–4, 5–8, 9–12, 13–16,
  17–18
Exclamations, 9–12, 18

H

Helping verbs, 99–102, 108

I

Irregular verbs, 91–94, 95–98,
  107

M

Main and helping verbs, 99–102, 108
Mechanics
  See Apostrophes; Capitalization;
   Commas; End marks; Punctuation;
   Titles *of People*

Grammar Practice Book
© Harcourt • Grade 2

N

Naming parts of sentences, 13–16, 18
Nouns
    capitalization of, 27–30, 31–34,
        35–36
    common, 19–22, 23–26, 35
    plural possessive, 45–48, 54
    proper, 27–30, 31–34, 35–36
    singular and plural, 19–22, 23–26,
        35–36
    singular possessive, 41–44, 53

P

Past-tense verbs, 81–84, 85–88, 90,
    91–94, 95–98, 107–108
Plural nouns, 23–26, 35
Plural possessive nouns, 45–48, 54
Possessive nouns, 41–44, 45–48,
    53–54
Predicates, 13–16, 18
Present-tense verbs, 73–76, 85–88,
    89, 91–94, 95–98
Pronouns, 49–52, 53–54
Proper nouns, 27–30, 31–34, 35–36
Punctuation
    abbreviations, 37–40, 53
    apostrophes in contractions,
        103–106, 108
    apostrophes in possessives, 41–44,
        45–48, 53–54
    end marks, 1–4, 5–8, 9–12, 13–16,
        17–18

Q

Questions, 5–8, 12, 17

S

Sentence Parts, 13–16, 18
Sentences, kinds of, 5–8, 9–12, 17–18
    commands, 9–12, 18
    exclamations, 9–12, 18
    questions, 5–8, 17–18
    parts of, 13–16
    statements, 1–4, 5–8, 17–18
Singular and plural nouns, 19–22,
    23–26, 35–36
Singular and plural pronouns, 49–52,
    54
Singular possessive nouns, 41–44, 53
Statements, 1–4, 17–18
Subjects, 13–16, 18
Subject-verb Agreement, 77–80,
    85–88, 89–90, 91–94, 95–98,
    99–102, 107–108

T

Telling parts of sentences, 13–16, 18
Tenses
    past-tense verbs, 81–84, 85–88, 90,
        91–94, 95–98, 107–108
    present-tense verbs, 73–76, 77–80,
        85–88, 89, 91–94, 95–98, 107

Grammar Practice Book
© Harcourt • Grade 2

Grammar Practice Book
© Harcourt • Grade 2